Original title:
The Arbor's Tale

Copyright © 2025 Creative Arts Management OÜ
All rights reserved.

Author: Kieran Blackwood
ISBN HARDBACK: 978-1-80566-670-7
ISBN PAPERBACK: 978-1-80566-955-5

The Heartwood Chronicles

In a forest full of chatter,
A squirrel slipped on some splatter.
The acorns rolled, oh what a sight,
He blushed and hid, feeling slight.

A wise old tree leaned in to say,
'You're the star of the show today!'
With branches wide, he offered cheer,
The squirrel giggled, 'I'll steer clear.'

With vines that wove a silly hat,
The tree grinned wide, it looked quite flat.
The critters danced beneath the boughs,
"To fashion's whim, we all say vows!"

An owl hooted into the night,
"Fashion faux pas? What a delight!"
The tree shrugged with leafy grace,
"Next time, squirrel, choose a better space."

Musings of a Weathered Trunk

Beneath the sky, I twist and bend,
With stories back to when I'd trend.
Once a young sapling, ripe with style,
Now I'm dressed in bark quite a while.

A chipmunk claimed my cozy nook,
Used my bark to write a book.
He scribbled tales of love and strife,
But lost his muse to lunchtime life.

The birds above discuss their flight,
While ants march on, a silly sight.
In dreams, I'm dancing, young and spry,
But here I sit, with time gone by.

Oh, how I envy the breeze's call,
That whispers sweet to one and all.
Yet here I am, with roots so deep,
I'll laugh at shadows, then I'll sleep.

The Dance of Dappled Light

Sunlight sparkles through the leaves,
The ground it tickles, oh, how it weaves.
A rabbit hops with grace and flair,
While shadows dance, without a care.

Each beam of light that touches ground,
Makes every critter twirl around.
With laughter bright, they prance and play,
Turning the mundane into a ballet.

A butterfly sips on dew so sweet,
While ants keep time with tiny feet.
In this bright ball, the branches sway,
Filling the world with joy and play.

When twilight casts a gentle glow,
They wind down softly, taking it slow.
The woods whisper tales of delight,
As stars emerge, and bid goodnight.

Lullabies for Lost Woods

In the depths where whispers dwell,
The trees spin yarns, all is well.
A hedgehog snores, snug as can be,
Dreaming of snacks beneath the tree.

The breeze hums soft a drowsy tune,
While crickets chirp beneath the moon.
Fireflies wink, like tiny stars,
Guiding lost souls, like supercars.

Once a wanderer, lost in thought,
Stumbled upon the tales they brought.
With every step, a giggle blooms,
As laughter echoes through the glooms.

So close your eyes and rest your head,
Let dreams whisk you where herbs are spread.
In lost woods warm, with a chuckle bright,
Lullabies twine through the velvet night.

A Haven of Green Dreams

In the garden, where the gnomes dance,
The squirrels plot their nutty romance.
Plants gossip low, they gossip high,
While bees make buzz that sounds like a sigh.

One tree thought it could brush the sky,
But tripped on roots, oh my, oh my!
The daisies chuckled, petals in a whirl,
As pine cones laughed, "Look at that girl!"

Under the sun, the worms have fun,
Playing hopscotch, just on the run.
With shades of green, the grass does gleam,
It's a riot here, in the dream team.

So join the laugh under leafy beams,
In this place where nothing's as it seems.
Nature's circus, wild and bright,
A funny world, pure delight!

In the Embrace of Nature's Arms

The trees wear hats, crafted from leaves,
Dancing to whispers, one truly believes.
The rocks tell tales of days gone past,
While sunlight giggles, the shadows cast.

A rabbit suggests a game of tag,
But tripped on roots, in a floppy rag.
While butterflies flirt, the ants parade,
With tiny drumsticks, they shimmy and sway.

Flowers wear shades, looking quite grand,
"Where's Berry the Badger?" asks one in the sand.
"Oh, he's napping! Let's play peek-a-boo!"
As the wind joins in, with a woo-hoo!

In nature's arms, laughter thrives,
Each day is silly, where joy derives.
So come take part, in this wild charm,
With every giggle, it's safe from harm!

Whispers of the Woodland

In the woods, where trees have a chat,
A poofy squirrel wears a fluffy hat.
"Did you hear about the funny frog?"
He croaks a joke, sided by a log.

Hedgehogs tumble, rolling down hills,
While mushrooms giggle, sharing silly thrills.
A wise old owl hoots with delight,
Cheering the critters, oh what a sight!

The creek babbles secrets, soft and loud,
As rabbits hop, proudly, straight and proud.
Each corner holds a jester's surprise,
Nature's laughter dances in the skies.

With vines that twist and twirl in glee,
Each path we walk is a frolic for free.
In this woodland realm, joy always calls,
A merry adventure where humor befalls!

Growth Rings of Time

Old trees tell tales, with rings so round,
Each year a story, each laugh a sound.
"Remember when the storm blew us east?"
The roots shake their heads, "What a feast!"

With mushrooms popping like party hats,
The ladybugs dance and wear their spats.
A wise old branch sways with a grin,
"Nature's a jest, let the fun begin!"

Caterpillars dream of future flight,
Counting the laughs in the moonlight.
"Oh, we were funny," one leaf does chime,
"Look at us now, all silly in rhyme!"

So here we gather, under the bough,
Where time is a prankster, right here and now.
A circle of laughter, forever spins,
In the growth rings of joy, life always wins!

Chronicles of the Whispering Branches

In the breeze, branches chatter,
Squirrels gossip, oh what a clatter!
Leaves throw shade on a sunbaked toad,
Who dreams of chill in a leafy abode.

Twigs jump as a pigeon prances,
Bark laughs as the woodpecker dances.
Acorns rolling, a game of chance,
Every critter joins in the silly romance.

Raccoons plot under the moon's glow,
Crafting schemes of the snacks they'll stow.
A racquetball made of lost nuts they claim,
Turns into a game, oh what a wild fame!

Laughter echoes through the wide woods,
Even the grumpy old owl feels good.
With every tickle of wind through the leaves,
Nature's giggles weave tales like these.

Tales from the Timbered Heart

Once a tree wore a parrot bright,
Chattering secrets all day and night.
Branches bent low with laughter so free,
Even the roots joined in for the spree.

A squirrel in shades thought it was cool,
Trying to teach the grass how to drool.
Frogs in the pond sang silly new tunes,
While turtles crouched, late for their prunes.

Bumblebees buzzing, a dance on high,
Won the hearts of the flowers nearby.
Each petal swayed as the buds took flight,
Joy blossomed fully, oh what a sight!

Evening wraps round, storytime's here,
The owls tell tales, and the crickets cheer.
Under the stars, the forest sings bright,
In their woodsy way, they bring such delight.

Songs of the Winding Vines

Vines twist and twirl, a party of green,
Whispering secrets like they're on screen.
A snail in a race, so slow and quite proud,
Challenges bumblebees buzzing aloud.

Mice hold a feast on a thick leafy bed,
Cheeses and crackers, oh, nothing but spread!
Spiders spin webs that shimmer and tease,
While ants march along, saying "Please, oh please!"

The moon peeks in, a curious guest,
Raccoons invite her to join their jest.
"Come dance with us under the starlit dew,"
Laughter erupts, as they all join the crew.

Mirth fills the air, a sweet, merry song,
In the dance of the night, nothing feels wrong.
Roots tap to the beat, as the trees sway, too,
In this realm of joy, the world feels brand new.

Beneath the Boughs of Time

Old trees tell tales in creaks and squeaks,
Of youthful days with adventurous peaks.
A brisk wind giggles through branches so wide,
Chasing lost leaves on a whimsical ride.

Nutty squirrels plan a grand heist at dawn,
With acorn hats looking quite posh and drawn.
They giggle and sneak with nuts in their cheeks,
A friendly heist that brings everyone freaks.

Grasshoppers grin, playing leapfrog with glee,
While snappy young turtles just wait by the tree.
The sun shines down, casting shadows so fun,
A merry spectacle, under sky's run!

As stars blink bright, with twinkling delight,
Creatures gather round, and share their best night.
In laughter and cheer, their spirits will climb,
For nothing beats joy 'neath the boughs of time.

Reveries of the Wildwood

In a grove where squirrels prance,
A chipmunk thinks it's time to dance.
With acorns bouncing off a tree,
He giggles 'Who will dance with me?'

The raccoons roll their eyes in glee,
While pondering their next big spree.
They'll raid the picnics, bring the snacks,
In woodland chaos, there are no lacks.

The owl hoots loudly, laughing now,
'What silly creatures, oh my wow!'
The fox joins in with a sly grin,
'Today's the day for mischief to begin!'

But when the sun begins to set,
The woodland antics, we'll forget.
So tuck in tight, dear creatures small,
Tomorrow, we'll have fun, after all!

Enchanted by the Forest's Breath

A bear rocks out to forest tunes,
While birds pollute the air with croons.
'What's that smell?' the bear does plead,
'Oh wait, it's just my berry seed!'

The mushrooms chuckle, swell with cheer,
As giggling trees lean in to hear.
The rabbits hop around the glen,
Turning summer's dance into a trend.

'Let's hold a jam, it'll be a blast!'
Cried out the deer, with hope so vast.
They pranced and twirled 'neath leafy crowns,
Creating laughter all around.

But soon the mischievous winds did blow,
They tangled fur, made loops that flow.
Yet through the chaos, they just laughed,
In magical woods, joy is the craft!

The Heartbeat of Each Season

In spring, the blooms wear silly hats,
While bees declare that they are brats.
They buzz about with laughter bright,
'We're here to keep the flowers light!'

Summer brings a sun-soaked snooze,
While critters play with silly shoes.
The frogs leap high with a splashy cheer,
'This pond is ours, come join us here!'

Autumn's leaves swirl like confetti,
'Catch me if you can!' says one, so petty.
Squirrels make piles, then jump right in,
They chuckle 'Ah, let the games begin!'

But winter's chill, it comes with style,
Snowflakes dance down, all the while.
A snowman winks, with carrot nose,
'Let's hold a feast, that's how it goes!'

The Wisdom of the Old Growth

In the forest, tall and wide,
Trees gossip, never hide.
Branches tickle, leaves all sway,
Roots, they dance in their own way.

Squirrels jest, a lively crew,
Planning pranks, just for you.
Old trunks chuckle, stories spun,
Nature's laughter—never done!

Birds exchange the latest news,
While shadows play in dappled hues.
Wisdom whispers through the bark,
Each ring a tale, a playful spark.

Fungi giggle 'neath the trees,
Spreading cheer with every breeze.
Nature's jesters, wise and spry,
In this green realm, laughter's nigh.

The Emissary of Evergreen Dreams

Evergreen with tales to weave,
Whispers float among the leaves.
Spruce so tall, perched up high,
Makes the clouds laugh and sigh.

Pinecones fall like jokers tossed,
Nature chuckles, never lost.
Little critters scurry around,
In this forest, joy is found.

Hooting owls, wise yet sly,
Crackin' jokes while passing by.
Even the sun joins the fun,
Winking down, it's number one!

Here in dreams of green so bright,
Laughter echoes, pure delight.
With each breeze, more tales arise,
Nature's giggles fill the skies.

Melodies of the Majestic Maple

Maple leaves in colors bold,
Sway and dance, their joys unfold.
Carpenter bees hum their tune,
As sunshine glistens like a boon.

Branches bending, bowing low,
They share secrets, don't you know?
With each rustle, a chuckling sound,
Nature's jokes are all around.

Sap flows sweet, a syrup stream,
Buzzing bees capture the dream.
Whimsy in every swirling breeze,
Maples laugh, and so do we.

Tap a tree, hear stories spill,
Nature's humor, always will.
So let's frolic, dance, and play,
With the maples, bright the day!

The Hearthstone of Nature's Stories

In the heart of woods, we gather round,
Listen close to the tales profound.
Rabbits chat of carrot's fame,
Foxes giggle, it's all a game.

The hearthstone warms with stories old,
Of mischief magic and legends bold.
Crickets chirp their night-time song,
Echoes of laughter, all night long.

Woodpeckers drum, creating beats,
The forest hums, with life it greets.
Tales of daring, foolish and bright,
Under the stars, it feels just right.

Gather close, let the laughs unfold,
Nature's hearth, a treasure to hold.
For in each story shared anew,
Lies the joy of me and you.

Conversations with the Wind

The wind whispers secrets, oh so sly,
Telling the trees just how to fly.
With giggles and chuckles, it swirls around,
Tickling the branches, a playful sound.

Leaves chat back, a rustling cheer,
"Can you keep it down? We're trying to hear!"
They gossip of clouds, and the rain's sweet kiss,
In a dance of laughter, nothing amiss.

Portrait of a Sturdy Oak

Behold the oak, so grand and stout,
With a grin on its bark, it shouts, "No doubt!"
Each knot a story, each ring a jest,
A sturdy fellow, never thinks of rest.

The squirrels clamor, making it their stage,
With acorn hats, they're full of rage.
"You're too old to dance," they tease with glee,
Oak just chuckles, saying, "Watch me be!"

The Life in a Leaf

A leaf strolled in, bright and bold,
Whispered to others, "Let's break the mold!"
With a twirl and a spin, it flips in the air,
"Catch me if you can, if you dare!"

The sun throws shade, just dressed in gold,
Leaf laughed aloud, feeling quite old.
"I dance with the breeze, not care for time,
Growing up's boring—this is my prime!"

Echoing the Ancients

Echoes of laughter from trees long gone,
Whisper tales of sunshine and dawn.
"Remember the days of thunderous cheer?"
They chuckle aloud, their voices clear.

The roots intertwine, in a cabaret,
With mushrooms applauding the wise old play.
"Who knew we'd thrive with such flair and style?"
The trees laugh together in a leafy smile.

Portrait of a Living Memory

Once upon a gusty breeze,
A squirrel wore a little cheese.
With every jump, he felt so spry,
As birds reviewed him from the sky.

The oak tree laughed, a mighty sound,
At nutty antics on the ground.
With branches swaying left and right,
It joined the show, a leafy sight.

Grasshoppers chirped their odes in tune,
While daisies danced beneath the moon.
Oh how they shared such joyful tales,
In whispers soft from blooming pales.

Then came a breeze with mischief found,
With tickles shared all around.
The memory stitched itself quite bold,
In giggles spun from stories old.

Conversations with the Rustling Leaves

Leaves chatter softly in the fall,
In leafy gossip, they enthrall.
"I saw a crow steal someone's snack!"
Nearby, a squirrel wore a hat, quite whack!

"Did you hear what the tree next door said?
'I'm getting old, I need a bed!'"
The birch laughed loud, in shades so bright,
While whispering pine just felt polite.

"Let's play a game, a rustle tag!
Catch me if you can!" said a bragged mag.
With flutters, they spread through the air,
Oh, what a mischief they'd declare!

As sunlight fades and shadows swoop,
They crack jokes about the morning's loop.
Nature's humor, light and free,
In every leaf, a comic spree.

Symphony of the Seasons' Change

Winter's tune was all a-blend,
With snowflakes dancing, no end.
The trees hummed low in frosty breath,
While critters played at the harvest's death.

Spring stepped in with a boisterous shout,
"Time to wake, no time for doubt!"
Buds popped up in a vibrant glee,
And critters cheered, "Just wait and see!"

Summer came with a sunny grin,
"Let's splash about, let the games begin!"
The flowers chuckled, in hues so bold,
In warmth and laughter, stories told.

Then autumn joined with a twinkling sigh,
"Isn't this fun? Oh me, oh my!"
With colors lost yet spirits high,
Each season's charm would never die.

Nature's Silent Witness

In the meadow, grass whispering dreams,
Nature chuckles, or so it seems.
A rabbit slips on a patch of clay,
And then does a dance, hip-hop ballet!

The creek giggles, rounded stones in tow,
As fish spin tales of stealthy flow.
"I saw you jump! You almost fell!"
"Not me," replied the frog, "I know it well!"

Sunbeam spies through the leafy dome,
Taking pictures, calling it home.
"Oh, look at that butterfly! What a sight!"
"Must've been up all day and night!"

With every rustle, laughter flies,
In nature's court, no truth denies.
The silent witness simply sees,
The joyful antics of critters with ease.

Starlit Canopy Stories

Under stars that twinkle bright,
Squirrels dance in sheer delight.
Branches sway with laughter loud,
Joining in the playful crowd.

Frogs in ties croak jokes in glee,
Telling tales on bended knee.
Owls hoot from their lofty seats,
As critters shuffle on their feet.

Fireflies flash like tiny lights,
Guiding rolling acorn fights.
Trees chuckle with a creaky sound,
As nature's humor spins around.

Beneath this canopy so wide,
Joyful moods cannot abide.
In this forest, glee is king,
And every creature loves to sing.

Lament of the Fallen Leaves

Leaves descend in swirling dance,
Whisper words of lost romance.
Breezes laugh, they swirl and sway,
As autumn steals the green away.

Each leaf wore a coat of cheer,
Now scattered, whispering their fear.
"Oh! Not ready to take a flight,
We'd rather stay and bask in light!"

Branches shake with chuckling glee,
"Time to go, you won't be free!"
But leaves roll down the winding lanes,
And gather, giggling like old friends.

In vibrant piles, they craft a bed,
Snagging kids who come to tread.
Yet as they crunch, the leaves can't grieve,
For laughter shines where they believe.

Ballad of the Twisted Roots

Roots that wiggle, roots that bend,
Twisting tales they love to send.
Sneaky tendrils chase the ants,
In muddy boots, they play their prance.

"Hey there buddy, caught you quick!
Your crumbs? We'll snatch them, just for kicks!"
Roots entwine with playful mirth,
Creating a dance upon the earth.

Unruly, they tangled and curled,\nMaking mazes in a world.
Spinning stories underground,
Where giggles and whispers abound.

"Watch your step, oh, look out there!
We might just trip you, if you dare!"
These joyful roots, with glee imbued,
Sing happy songs—nature's mood!

Serenity in the Silent Grove

In a grove where silence reigns,
Nature hums with joyful strains.
Trees hold secrets, quiet jokes,
Amongst the shadows, laughter pokes.

Mossy stones wear grins so wide,
As sunlight captures blooms inside.
"Shh," says the brook with splashing cheer,
"Nature's fun, yet we all can hear!"

Whispers float on breezy trails,
Where chipmunks tell their tiny tales.
In quietude, the giggles rise,
Nature's humor in disguise.

So find your peace among the smiles,
Join the chatter, walk the miles.
In this grove, where fun is found,
Silence sings, the joy abounds.

The Spirit of the Dancing Branches

In a grove of giggles, trees sway and prance,
With whispers of laughter, they join in the dance.
Branches dressed in hats made of leaves,
Jiving to tunes that the breeze weaves.

Squirrels swing by, with acorns in hand,
Winking at joggers, oh isn't it grand?
Rabbits do twirls while the owls hoot in glee,
Nature's own rhythm, a merry jamboree.

Mushrooms are clapping, their caps up so high,
While flower buds giggle, they can't help but try.
The sun slips a peek through a curtain of green,
Shining on frolics, a whimsical scene.

When moonlight arrives, the show doesn't cease,
Now shadows do tango, oh what a release!
With snickers and snorts, all the creatures unite,
In a nightscape of wonder, till morning's first light.

Ballads of the Shaded Glade

Beneath the broad boughs, a plot thickens well,
With giggling fawns and a mischievous spell.
The grass sings a tune, as critters all cheer,
Weaving tales of folly, we gather near.

Beetles in tuxedos, a grand soirée,
Invite every creature to come out and play.
With a hop and a skip, they spin in delight,
While fireflies flash like tiny starlight.

The wise old owl offers puns from his perch,
As chattering chipmunks break out in a lurch.
Each tale wrapped in laughter, a tickle of fun,
Creating a ballad, when day's nearly done.

So raise up your cups of sweet nectar and cheer,
For in shaded glades, there's laughter, my dear.
In the heart of the woods, where spirits take flight,
We'll dance through the evening, joy flooding the night.

Mysteries Woven in Green

In the heart of the forest, curious waits,
As vines knit their secrets through twisted old gates.
From squirrels' sly whispers and foxes' sly schemes,
Unraveling laughter is more than it seems.

With ferns as their curtains, the jokes start to rise,
As daisies throw shade with their playful surprise.
Branches twist tales that are just too absurd,
Every pause taken, a chance for a word.

Laughter erupts from the moss-covered logs,
While hedgehogs applaud, and the frogs join in cogs.
A fox with a grin whispers riddles so slick,
Telling the woods where the magical trick.

As dawn stretches wide, the giggles disperse,
Yet echoes remain in the greenery's verse.
So linger awhile, where tales intertwine,
In the mysteries woven where spirits align.

Veils of Mist and Memory

In the cool of the morn, where the mist plays along,
The trees share their tales, where giggles belong.
With soft, whispering breezes, they gossip and sigh,
While the shadows all chuckle and join in the cry.

A bunny with swagger, a wisecrack to share,
"Why did the leaf drop? Just to show that it's bare!"
With petals a-sway, and dandelions laugh,
The sun peeks in softly at the woodland's half-staff.

Mushrooms, like hats, with their cap-tipping flair,
Join in the jest, as they dance without care.
Each blossom a jester, in this green frolic fair,
Where mist serves as curtains, and memories share.

So let's twirl with the fern-folk and spin in the glow,
For the day may be fleeting, but laughter will flow.
In veils of soft mist, where the past meets the fun,
We'll weave all our stories till the setting of sun.

The Dance of the Branching Paths

In the woods, a squirrel pranced,
Twisting left, then right, he danced.
With acorns flying high and wide,
He made the trees his joyful slide.

A raccoon joined with a silly grin,
He shuffled in, all set to spin.
Together they twirled in leafy delight,
While birds above cheered, what a sight!

The branches swayed to a tune so bright,
Nature's orchestra, pure delight.
The sun peeked through the canopy,
As if to say, "Come join the spree!"

But oh, the owl up high did hoot,
"Watch where you step, don't lose your boot!"
They toppled down in giggles and plays,
And the forest chuckled for days and days.

Echoes of Nature's Heart

In the glade, a frog did croak,
With echoes loud, he surely woke.
"Is anyone there?" he hollered out,
And bushes rustled all about.

A rabbit popped up, ears so tall,
"Just making sure you're not in thrall!"
The frog replied, "I'm just a sound,
Let's riddle where the jokes abound!"

The echo replied, "I'm here for fun,
Sing a tune, let's all run!"
So they croaked and hopped with glee,
While birds perched clucked in harmony.

They spun in circles, caught in jest,
Nature's chorus, over the rest.
With every laugh, the woods did cheer,
Echoing humor loud and clear.

Fables from the Forest Floor

Once a beetle wore a crown of leaves,
While telling tales that spun like weaves.
He claimed he was king of all he saw,
   Though really, he fit in a tiny straw.

A snail chimed in with wisdom old,
"I heard you brag, but here's the gold.
You're lovely, dear, but slow and shy,
No need for crowns when you're spry!"

A laughter burst from the bushes near,
As a chipmunk piped up, full of cheer.
"Let's skip the titles and just be pals,
We're creatures of fun, not noble gals!"

So fables spread throughout the glen,
Of beetles, snails, and good-natured men.
They feasted on laughter, oh what a score,
   In the heart of the forest, forever more.

Heartbeats in the Hollow

Deep in the hollow, a bear gave a grin,
His belly rumbled, let the feasting begin!
With berries aplenty, a feast to explore,
He danced round the tree like never before.

A hedgehog rolled in, spikes all aglow,
"Can I join in, or is that a no?"
The bear laughed hard, "Roll on in, my friend,
Let's make this party the best without end!"

They jived with the flowers, in rhythm and rhyme,
While critters crept in, unafraid of time.
A party developed under stars so bright,
With heartbeats thumping through the magical night.

But down by the creek, the fish felt left out,
So they splashed and twirled with a great, big shout.
And all through the hollow, you'd hear their delight,
'Cause in nature's embrace, it's all pure delight!

The Silent Sentinel

In the park, a tree stood tall,
With branches spread, it tried to call.
Whispers flew in winds so breezy,
But squirrels found it all too cheesy.

Rooted firmly in the ground,
It hoped for friends, but none around.
A bird perched high, with chirp so spry,
Said, "Go on, don't be shy, give it a try!"

Every season, through rain or shine,
Its bark held tales of a time divine.
Yet leaves fell down, a laugh or two,
"Guess this trunk can't carry through!"

Still, it stood with humor bright,
As dusk brought chill, it found delight.
"Catch me if you can, I won't stand still,
Just watch as I wiggle, I've got the thrill!"

Seasons of the Timbered Grove

Spring brought blooms, a floral jest,
With bees that buzzed in every nest.
The trees would dance in gentle sway,
While leaves cried out, "Hooray, hooray!"

Summer's sun, a laughter fest,
Where shade was sought, but ants were guests.
They marched in lines, so proud and racy,
Warring over crumbs, all so racy!

Autumn's hues, a comic show,
As branches bare put on a glow.
"Oops! Did I drop that? Oooh, my bad!"
Leaves laughed and tumbled, what a fad!

Winter's chill, a frozen breath,
Made trees look grim, like they were death.
But snowflakes danced, "We're just like you,
Here for fun, all white and new!"

Leaves of Yesterday

Once bright and green, now all a mess,
Old leaves giggled, "What a dress!"
They rustled tales of days gone by,
Where sunshine flashed, and time flew high.

The wind would tease, "Come float with me!"
"Not ready yet!" they'd shout with glee.
As autumn came, they made a fuss,
"Time to jump, no need to rush!"

One leaf complained of too much sun,
"Just soak it in, it's far from done!"
With every gust, they'd twist and turn,
Learning life's dance with every churn.

At twilight's call, they whispered low,
"Let's write a book on how we glow!"
A memoir of leaves, so bold and bright,
Who laughed at change, and took to flight.

Twilight among the Saplings

Saplings stood like tiny guards,
Each sporting leaves, like colorful cards.
Twilight fell, and shadows danced,
As they pranced around, in a playful trance.

"I'm taller!" one would proudly boast,
"I'm stronger!" said another, with a toast.
In giggles soft, they shared their dreams,
Of reaching high, like forest teams.

A curious fox peeked through the trees,
"What's this ruckus? Hey, where's my cheese?"
The saplings laughed, "We have no food,
But join us now, and change your mood!"

And so they played in evening's glow,
As stars blinked down, "What a show!"
In silly games, friendships grew,
In twilight's hush, they giggled anew.

Memory of the Ageless Tree

Once a branch held my old sock,
That tree just giggled, what a shock.
Squirrels laughed, they had a ball,
In the sprightly shade of the tallest wall.

Round the trunk, we danced with glee,
All thanks to that wise old tree.
It whispered tales, oh so absurd,
Of gossiping leaves and a cheeky bird.

Raccoons joined, making a fuss,
"What's a tree without a break for us?"
I climbed up high, feeling spry,
But tripped on roots, oh me, oh my!

So here's to trees, with humor rife,
Making memories that add to life.
Each branch a laugh, each leaf a cheer,
Those ageless trees, forever dear.

The Meeting Under the Moonlit Canopy

Under the glow of the silver beam,
We gathered beneath a leafy theme.
The owls hooted, in robes so fine,
Telling jokes that crossed the vine.

A raccoon wore a tiny crown,
Declaring he was the king in town.
We all giggled, the shadows danced,
In that moonlit grove, all were entranced.

The mushrooms swayed, they were quite bold,
Singing tunes that never got old.
With every note, the branches swayed,
As laughter erupted and memories made.

With a flick of leaves, it was time to go,
We promised to meet, just so we know.
Though the moon was waning, our spirits soared,
One funny night, among nature adored.

Odyssey of the Forgotten Woods

In woods so thick, where stories thrive,
A frog wore goggles, and felt alive.
He claimed to be an ancient sage,
With the wisdom of a lively page.

The trees leaned in with bated breath,
As critters pondered life and death.
But all they learned was how to prank,
And make that old pond their festive bank.

A squirrel showed off his acorn stash,
Declaring it was worth a splash.
He slipped and fell, but what a show,
A cannonball leap into the low flow!

So here's to the fun in the woods so green,
Where laughter echoes, and joy is seen.
Though forgotten by some, they now delight,
In the odysey of woods, every night!

The Hushed Songs of Autumn

As autumn leaves began to fall,
The trees would whisper, oh so small.
They hummed a tune, quiet yet bright,
In the hush of twilight, it felt just right.

A chipmunk pranced, with acorns five,
Singing along, feeling alive.
His voice cracked, but who could care,
When everyone joined in, a lovely affair.

The foliage painted a vibrant show,
As breezes teased, and whispers flowed.
They joked of winters, the chill up ahead,
While squirrels plotted, and mischief spread.

So let's gather in this autumn air,
And join the songs without a care.
In the hush of nature, let joy prevail,
For laughter rings in every tale.

Roots of Memory

In the garden of thoughts, they grow,
Each worm a whisper, each seed a show.
Laughter rings out from the leafy knoll,
Silly stories that tickle the soul.

A squirrel in pants, oh what a sight!
Jumps for acorns, filled with delight.
The flowers giggle, the daisies sway,
As the trees gossip of their heyday.

With roots intertwined like a cheeky dance,
They sway to the rhythm of life's chance.
A nutty family reunion spree,
Where pinecones bounce, wild and free.

Every shadow seems to wear a grin,
As if the earth's chuckling from within.
In this woodland circus, oh what a thrill,
Roots of memory, eternal and still.

Echoes of the Forest Floor

Amongst the ferns, the whispers play,
Rustling secrets in a silly way.
The mushrooms giggle, the toadstools shout,
Echoes of laughter flutter about.

A raccoon in slippers thinks he's a star,
Practicing tricks, he's raising the bar.
With every tumble and twisty flop,
The forest erupts, will he ever stop?

Beneath the leaves, the critters engage,
In a slapstick act, they're turning the page.
A beetle in shades, and oh so proud,
Guides the mischief with a laugh so loud.

The forest floor, a stage of glee,
Where every creature's a wannabe.
In echoes of joy, they find their score,
As nature conducts from the leafy floor.

A Symphony of Leaves

A breeze strums softly through branches high,
Leaves dance along, they twist and fly.
Each rustle a note in the melody spun,
Nature's orchestra, a riot of fun.

The wind a maestro, with flair so bold,
Conducting the tales of the shy and the old.
With a flick of a twig and a flap of a wing,
The Critter Choir starts to sing!

A cacophony of chirps, a tap of a foot,
The frogs take the stage in their slick little suit.
While the bumblebees hum in a buzzing ring,
Join in the jig, let the laughter spring.

A symphony played on the forest stage,
Where every leaf turns a joyful page.
With roots and boughs in this funny dance,
Every creature sways, lost in a trance.

Shadows Beneath the Boughs

Under thick canopies, shadows play tricks,
A jesting raccoon with his sly little flicks.
He hides in the dusk, peeking with glee,
Waiting for squirrels to dart past a tree.

The wise old owl hoots, "What's this surprise?"
While giggling chipmunks roll, oh how they rise.
In the twilight glow, they leap and they bound,
The laughter of nature, a whimsical sound.

Twisted tales of mischief unfold,
Where secrets are whispered, and laughter is gold.
The branches all tremble, from hearty delight,
As shadows cavort into the night.

Under the boughs, where stories collide,
In that playful space where the shadows reside.
Every rustle and giggle, a moment to keep,
In the heart of the woods, where memories leap.

The Sundering of Seasons

Winter wore its frosty crown,
While Spring laughed and tumbled down.
Summer strutted, sun ablaze,
Fall danced in a leaf-clad daze.

Icicles and blossoms collide,
A tree stood gaping, open wide.
"Can we all just get along?"
It asked, stifling yawns in song.

With every gust, the seasons bickered,
Frosty fingers poked and snickered.
Yet amid the playful quarrels,
Giggles echoed through the spirals.

So under branches green and wide,
The seasons laughed, and none could hide.
For every twig's a punchline found,
In nature's joke, with roots unbound.

Whispers of the Old Oak

An old oak stood, with wisdom deep,
Telling secrets it couldn't keep.
Squirrels giggled, perched so high,
"Did you hear the fox? Oh my!"

"Last week he wore a silly hat,
Thought he was so cool and fat!"
The branches shook, the leaves all swayed,
As laughter rolled, the wise oak played.

Birds chimed in on every jest,
With chirps and tweets; they did their best.
"Oh, the tales I could recite,
About that raccoon's late-night bite!"

And there, beneath the leafy dome,
Friends gathered, feeling right at home.
With every laugh, the oak then swayed,
Crafting tales that never frayed.

Beneath the Canopy's Veil

Beneath the leaves, a picnic spread,
Gnomes and fairies shared their bread.
"Did you grab my sandwich, please?
You know I'm quick, I take with ease!"

A rabbit hopped, with ears a-flop,
Said, "Hey, who's got the carrot crop?"
The ants rolled in, on tiny legs,
With sassy strides, like furry kegs.

"Sorry, mate, the crows just swooped,
They think it's us, they think we scooped!"
They chuckled loud, each story spun,
As grasshoppers joined in the fun.

With giggles echoing through the air,
The creatures danced without a care.
In nature's realm, the playful jest,
Made every moment feel the best.

Stories in the Gnarled Branches

Gnarled branches told of times gone by,
When trees wore hats of cotton candy sky.
"Remember when the winds did howl?
That daffodil turned into a fowl!"

Laughter burst from bark so thick,
"Just look at that old willow's trick!"
The elder tree, with leaves askew,
Swore by roots it once flew too.

"On windy days, I'd soar up high,
But only when I'd catch a sigh!"
Every leaf dropped hints of lore,
Of woodland pranks and tales of yore.

The weird and wild filled the air,
With every twist, a tale laid bare.
In every creak, a chuckle rose,
Within those branches, joy still flows.

A Tapestry of Bark

In the forest, trees wear hats,
A mix of acorns and some chats.
Squirrels giggle, on branches sway,
Sharing secrets of the day.

Leaves gossip as the breezes play,
Whispering tales of the old bark way.
A Robin laughs, 'Oh what a sight!'
As the sun dips, painting the night.

A raccoon dances, showing its flair,
While fireflies twinkle, unaware.
A woodpecker's knock is a drumbeat loud,
In this leafy, jubilant crowd.

Caterpillars dream in their silk cocoon,
Wishing to flutter beneath the moon.
With all this joy, it's hard to sleep,
In the tapestry where secrets seep.

Guardians of the Verdant Realm

In the kingdom of leafy hues,
Guardians dance, and shake their shoes.
The owls wear spectacles, wise and grand,
Quipping puns that are quite unplanned.

A hedgehog jests, 'I'm pointy but sweet!'
Chasing butterflies on tiny feet.
The moss giggles and sways with cheer,
While the bushes cackle, "We aren't here!"

Frogs croak in tune—a wet serenade,
While bumblebees buzz, plans they made.
Together they ward off nighttime fears,
With laughter that bubbles, ringing in ears.

Roots laugh deep, holding tales untold,
Of all the pranks that the forest holds.
The trees bow low, a comical scene,
In this realm where all things are green!

The Unseen Roots of Life

Beneath the ground where shadows cling,
The roots make jokes, a funny string.
They tickle worms who wriggle and giggle,
Spreading laughter, like a soft wiggle.

The fungi chuckle, dress like clowns,
Making merry in muddy crowns.
Tiny ants share crumbs they stole,
Orchard of laughter, that's their goal.

In this hidden world, mischief brews,
As beetles play dress-up in sparkly shoes.
With whispers of fun flowing through earth,
It's a raucous party—a root's rebirth.

Echoes of joy rise up like steam,
From the unseen roots, a whimsical dream.
In life's tangled dance, all is bright,
As critters jive 'neath the moonlight.

Beneath the Twilight Canopy

Beneath the trees, where shadows merge,
A raccoon with a mask starts to surge.
"Hiding from you, it's part of the game,
But find me quick, I'm tired of fame!"

The crickets chirp like seasoned pros,
Quipping jokes as the evening glows.
Fireflies flaunt their tiny lights,
"Follow us! Let's race through the nights!"

A badger trips over a crooked root,
Landing soft in his fluffy suit.
The lizards laugh, they can't contain,
As the owl hoots, "Oh, not again!"

As stars peek down, like curious eyes,
The laughter echoes, under the skies.
In this twilight world of giggly cheer,
Nature's laughter, forever near.

Whispers of the Willows

In a grove where willows sway,
The squirrels throw a nut buffet.
Chirping birds all sing in tune,
While frogs croak like they're on a dune.

Branching out with leafy hats,
The rabbits dance and juggle mats.
A raccoon steals a picnic treat,
And all agree it's quite a feat.

The wise old owl gives a hoot,
Joining in, he hoots, then scoot.
With laughter echoing through the air,
Nature's jesters, a lively fair.

So if you wander through this scene,
Expect a show that's unforeseen.
With every rustle, laugh, and cheer,
You'll find the forest's charm is clear.

Portrait of a Resilient Oak

In a field stands a mighty oak,
With branches strong, it loves a joke.
Its acorns drop with plopping sounds,
As critters laugh while rolling 'rounds.

The wind will whistle, twist, and tease,
Tickling leaves with gentle breeze.
Yet, unbothered, the oak will sway,
Saying, "Bring it on, it's just a play!"

Pigeons perch and tell their tales,
Of squirrels pulling off wild fails.
Each wrinkle in the bark can tell,
Of all the laughs and stories well.

A portrait painted in the sun,
Where humor dances, just for fun.
In nature's gallery so wide,
The oak stands proud, full of pride.

Chronicles of the Seasonal Shifts

Springtime's bloom brings much delight,
Flowers bloom, a colorful sight.
But sneaky bees with wiggly dance,
Get floral folks into a trance.

Summer sun, oh what a tease,
Icicles turn to dripping freeze.
Frogs in pools with splashes bold,
Compete for laughs—oh, behold!

Autumn's leaves begin to fall,
A crunchy carpet covers all.
The critters jump in joy, oh bliss,
Making piles to roll in, not miss.

Winter comes with snowy schemes,
The trees are wrapped in frosty dreams.
Kids on sleds shout with elation,
As nature plays in fun fascination.

Legends Carved in Bark

Upon the trunk, a story's told,
In carvings that are brave and bold.
A heart and initials etched with glee,
To tell of love from you to me.

Each notch and groove reveals a jest,
Of woodland creatures trying their best.
A bear attempted a dance so grand,
But tripped on roots, thus took a stand!

The tales of yore that trees can share,
Of bad puns made by the woodland hare.
With giggles growing round the base,
These legends bring a merry trace.

So gather 'round, let's read the signs,
Where laughter blooms in twisted lines.
In every bark, a funny spark,
The woods are alive, a joyful lark!

Signposts in Nature's Story

A squirrel holds a tiny sign,
Pointing to acorns, oh so fine.
With all his chatter and quick spins,
He'll guide you where the foraging begins.

The birds are tweeting, full of jest,
With mischief notes, they jest and jest.
A robin warns of coming rain,
But it's just a dive-bombing game they've lain.

The trees nod at tales we share,
Whispering breezes in the air.
Maple giggles, a cozy friend,
Swaying along till the day's end.

Under their shade, laughter blooms,
Nature's jesters, wearing costumes.
All the critters join the dance,
In this woodsy, wild circumstance.

Roots in the Fabric of Time

Deep down below, the roots conspire,
A rumor swap, a secret choir.
They pull the soil in playful fights,
And tickle worms with their funny bites.

The oak tells tales of ancient oak,
Of bugs that dance and trees that joke.
"Did you hear the one of the tree that flew?"
The roots all chuckle, "Oh, yes, it's true!"

Branches above roll their leafy eyes,
At roots below with their sly replies.
It's all a game in nature's play,
As roots and leaves make jokes each day.

Time spins on, with giggles entwined,
In the earth's embrace, we're humor-lined.
Every knot and gnarled twist,
Holds laughter wrapped in nature's mist.

Celebrations of the Swaying Branches

Branches sway to a breezy tune,
Dancing wildly, morning to moon.
With cicadas singing, oh what a sight,
Leaves flip and flop in pure delight.

A party among the fluttering leaks,
With giggling squirrels and clucking beaks.
"Pass me the nuts!" yells a chubby blue jay,
While below, the daisies join in the fray.

Twisting limbs, they spread the cheer,
Each swipe and swoosh brings laughter near.
Nature's raves beneath the sky,
As pollen drifts in a merry hi-five.

Celebrations held in shade and sun,
With nature's jesters, we laugh and run.
The joy flows free, no big demands,
In the sway of branches, life expands.

Tales of the Life Giver

Once there lived a tree, so jolly,
With branches bent from all the folly.
He grew up tall, but oh, so wide,
With roots that tangled and caused much pride.

Every spring, he threw a bash,
With flowers blooming in a flash.
The bees arrived to hum their tune,
As squirrels danced beneath the moon.

"Would you like a fruit?" he'd cheerfully sing,
"Or perhaps a nut for your funny fling?"
The critters gathered, hearts ablaze,
In the tales spun through laughter's maze.

From peeling bark to twinkling eyes,
Life's antics hide under the skies.
A life giver, filled with mirth,
Hearts entwined in nature's birth.

Whispers of the Ancient Grove

In the shade of the tree, where squirrels convene,
A wise old owl plots, wearing glasses so keen.
He hoots at the moon with a poet's delight,
While the leaves giggle softly, through day and through night.

The raccoons hold meetings, with snacks on their plates,
Debating which tree could host the best fates.
One claims it's the oak with a trunk like a tank,
While others propose it's the maple's fine prank.

A beetle rolls dice on a wide mushroom cap,
To see if his luck can escape from the trap.
But when he gets stuck, it's a comical sight,
As ants start a chant, "He's our court jester tonight!"

So through twisted branches, laughter will rise,
With secrets of nature hidden in sighs.
In this playful grove where the fauna amuses,
Life's riddles unwind with the oddest excuses.

Secrets Beneath the Canopy

Under thick branches, dreams flourish and sway,
A hedgehog slips on his tortoise's way.
He fumbles and tumbles, a pitiful sight,
While the crickets all chuckle at their clumsy knight.

A raccoon with flair sets up shop in a tree,
Selling acorn hats for a small fee.
With a wink and a nod, he calls out, 'Step right!'
His fashion's outrageous, though the look is a fright!

The owls hold a quiz, on who's the best flyer,
Contestants lose feathers, no one will retire.
With wings flapping wildly, they bump and collide,
So much for the winner, they all just abide.

Giggling vines weave tales spun with delight,
In this playful theatre, day turns into night.
For beneath the green blanket, secrets reside,
In a world of whimsy where laughter won't hide.

Shadows Among the Roots

Beneath the old roots, where mushrooms go creep,
Lies a gopher who dreams of the hills, oh so steep.
He plans to break free, but oh, what a slog,
As he gets sidetracked by a curious frog.

The shadow of breezes carries whispers around,
While a snail in a hurry plows through the ground.
He mutters and grumbles, 'I'm late for my race!'
With a pace so slow, it's a sitting duck chase.

The ants throw a barbecue, pulled weeds on a plate,
With diners so tiny, it's a grand banquet fate.
They dance 'round the flames, in a woodland parade,
And toast to the bugs who are never afraid!

So shadows will linger, with stories to tell,
Of critters and chuckles and odd games they sell.
In the dance of the roots, with giggles in tow,
There's fun in the flora, where wild jokes can grow.

Echoes of the Leafy Kingdom

In the leafy kingdom where laughter takes flight,
A peacock struts proudly, with feathers so bright.
He sings out loud, but the tune's quite absurd,
As the finches all mock—'Now that's truly unheard!'

The butterflies gossip as they flit to and fro,
Trading secrets and giggles in a vibrant glow.
They chatter and flutter, like whispers in air,
While the daisies all nod, with a delicate flair.

A turtle recites lines from his favorite book,
But he keeps losing track, with each little crook.
His friends start to yawn, 'Oh dear, make it swift!'
As the dragonflies feast on his storytelling gift.

From rustling branches to the softest breeze,
The echoes of humor weave tales with such ease.
In this leafy domain where joy knows no end,
The heartbeat of nature is laughter, my friend.

A Tapestry of Twisted Roots

In the woodland where squirrels play,
Knots and twists lead funny astray.
Branches dance in silly prance,
Rooted friends in a wobbly stance.

Bark wears a grin, it's quite absurd,
A wise old tree suggests a bird.
They laugh about acorn dreams,
And share their sunlight, or so it seems.

Whispers tell of a leaf gone rogue,
Crafting hats from morning fog.
Fungi chorus with giggling glee,
While shadows play hide and seek with me.

So take a stroll, don't be aloof,
Join in the jokes, under green roof.
Each root a tale, each leaf a jest,
In this merry grove, we're all guests.

Chronicle of the Timeless Trees

Once a tree had dreams of flight,
Tried to grow wings, oh what a sight!
Branches flailed in a gusty breeze,
Leaves would giggle, 'Drop to your knees!'

Another claimed it knew the past,
Wrote stories in rings, but none could last.
Whispering winds stole every lore,
How could a breeze write tales any more?

A woodpecker, mighty and bold,
Knocked on the trunk with tales of old.
The echo laughed, what a silly sound,
As trees swayed joyfully 'round and 'round.

So gather 'round, you readers keen,
For tales of trees like you've never seen.
In groves where laughter tickles the bark,
There's humor and wisdom—just look for the spark!

The Sanctuary of Shade

Under the boughs where laughter rings,
Frogs don toads as queens and kings.
The sunlight plays tricks, here and there,
While branches weave a mischievous air.

Chipmunks with smiles, they chit and chat,
Debating who's fluffier, dog or cat.
Twists and turns of a gnarled limb,
Each shadow dances, each moment a whim.

Sunbeams shoot like arrows of gold,
Warmed by giggles, not too bold.
A picnic shared with ants on parade,
In the cool comfort, sweet shade's made.

So come find a patch, let's all unwind,
Where every chuckle's a tie that binds.
In the garden of giggles, you'll want to stay,
The sanctuary of shade calls, come play!

Heartbeats of the Old Wood

In the heart of the woods, where chuckles bloom,
Trees exchange pranks, dispelling gloom.
An ancient oak boasts of age-old gags,
While younger sprouts roll in leafy rags.

A squirrel juggles acorns with flair,
While the chattering crows utter a dare.
Whispers of wisdom float through the air,
As roots wiggle while they pretend to care.

Every knotted branch holds an old wise tale,
Of a green frog who tried to sail.
Alongside a brook with a bubbly laugh,
Water joins in, sharing its path.

In the symphony of rustling leaves,
Heartbeats of wood make us believe.
So if you wander and hear the cheer,
Know the old wood's humor is always near!

The Chronicles of the Weathered Bark

Once a tree thought it could dance,
But tripped on roots, what a chance!
The squirrels laughed, they took a peek,
As branches nodded, so to speak.

The sun said, "Hey, don't feel so blue!"
You're more than wood, you're quite the view.
A bird chimed in with a joyful squawk,
"Just sway with me, let's take a walk!"

The wise old moss, with a chuckle low,
Whispered tales of storms and snow.
Through seasons thick, and summers thin,
The laughter grew, deep down within.

So here's to trees, with all their quirks,
Wobbling like they're in the jerks.
Rooted deep, they still have fun,
In the forest shade, they jump and run!

The Tapestry of Twigs

In the woodland twigs had a fair,
They wore little hats, stirred up the air.
Each twig a tip, a twist, a turn,
Learning to dance was the goal they yearn.

A pine poked fun, his needles pricked,
"Join my conga, let's get kicked!"
The oaks just chuckled, looked quite grand,
While willows swayed like they had planned.

A chorus arose, the woodland song,
"Twirl like a leaf, you can't go wrong!"
With acorns bouncing, they hopped about,
In their twiggy outfits, they laughed out loud.

So raise a toast to the playful crowd,
In leafy attire, they danced unbowed.
With each silly step, they felt alive,
In the forest's heart, they thrived and jived!

Succor of the Shaded Trunk

A chubby trunk sat cool in shade,
With stories of storms that had freely played.
The critters gathered, eyes full of glee,
As roots spun yarns of what they could see.

"There once was a storm," one young oak said,
"That sent all my branches right over my head!"
"Then what happened next?" squealed a tiny hare,
"Did you fight back the gale? Did you dare?"

The trunk just chuckled with earth-tone grace,
"I leaned with the wind, kept a slow pace.
Then all of you critters, ran for a hide,
While I held my ground, oh what a ride!"

The laughter echoed, a warm little thrill,
In the dappled greens, every heart did fill.
So cheers to the trunk, the wise gentle sage,
With tales of folly that never age!

Fables in the Forest's Embrace

In the forest glade, there's mischief afoot,
Where rabbits wear shoes and squirrels wear soot.
Their fables are wild, as wild can be,
"Who will win, the nut or the tree?"

A hedgehog joined, his quills all akimbo,
Said, "I'll tell you tales of my friend, the limbo!
He danced through the night, oh what a sight,
While owls cheered him on in evening light."

Then came the fox with a grin so sly,
"Let's wager a dance, who'll flutter and fly?"
With giggles and grins, they bounded around,
In woodland laughter, no sorrow found.

So here in the glen, life tiptoes with grace,
Mischief abounds in this magical place.
As creatures collide in joyous embrace,
Fables unfold with a funny old face!

The Legacy of the Elder Tree

In a forest green, an elder stood,
With stories of mischief, it misunderstood.
Squirrels would giggle, as acorns would fall,
The wise old trunk chuckled, 'I meant none at all!'

Birds would come over to gather and sing,
While the branches would sway, like a grand puppet string.
'Come here, little critters, let's dance in the breeze!'
The tree threw a party, as its leaves did tease.

But when autumn came knocking, the party was done,
With all of its friends quietly having their fun.
They laughed as they scattered, what a sight to behold,
With acorns in hats and their stories retold.

Now it stands tall, with a grin so wide,
A legend of laughter, with roots full of pride.
As seasons continue, it's still full of glee,
In the heart of the woods, like a big comedy.

Roots of Resilience

From tiny seeds sprout, with ambitions so bold,
Twisted and turned, but never controlled.
The roots would debate on who grew the most,
As snails would pass by, throwing shade with a boast.

Life's teasing performance in soil so vast,
Brought laughter galore, in a gathering amassed.
Every worm shared secrets of tunnels below,
While daisies above giggled in sun's warm glow.

But one day a breeze gave a shiver and shake,
The roots called a meeting, 'For goodness' sake!
If we're all connected, let's laugh this off quick,
It's just nature's way of playing a trick!'

Through storms and through droughts, they danced and they cheered,
Their resilience a comedy that no one had feared.
A root is a friend when the weather is tough,
With humor at hand, they would always be enough.

Flourish of the Fragrant Blossoms

In a garden so bright, the blossoms would joke,
Chatting with bee buddies, a laugh always woke.
'Hey dandelions, quit blowing your fluff,
We've got big plans, and they're quite tough!'

They'd swirl in the wind with a fragrant delight,
Winking at butterflies in pure sunlight.
'Watch out for the bumblebees buzzing near,
They might steal our nectar and pop up with cheer!'

The peonies giggled, 'We're dressed to impress,
With perfumes so sweet, it's a floral success!'
While tulips, so proud, flaunted colors so bright,
'Can we get a little sunshine, it's a fabulous sight!'

Each blossom contributed its flair and its fun,
A bouquet of laughter, under the sun.
Together they painted a scene oh-so-cool,
In the garden of giggles, where life is the fuel.

A Soliloquy in Sap

Oh sap, my dear friend, in a world full of trees,
You're the sweetest of stories, filling up with ease.
You trickle and chuckle, with laughter you flow,
The squirrels gather round, for your comedy show.

'What's the deal with bark, why's it all rough?'
Tree trunks nuzzle in, 'It's just nature's tough stuff!'
With knots in their wood and limbs barely free,
They'd share all their secrets, with vibrant glee.

And when spring arrives, the buds start to dance,
With blades of green grass, it's a whimsical prance.
'Let's bloom, let's shine, like it's the last call,
Life's too short to pout, let's have some fun after all!'

So here's to the sap, the glue of the woods,
In the laughter of trees, we find all the goods.
Let the canopies giggle, let the critters be spry,
For in every tall tale, nature loves to fly.

An Echo of Leafy Dreams

In a grove where nuts do laugh,
Squirrels spin their acorn craft.
Leaves gossip in the gentle breeze,
'Trust us, we're the buzzing bees!'

Branching tales of owls so wise,
Who misunderstand the moonlit cries.
'Was that a hoot or just a sneeze?'
They ponder under swaying trees.

The butterflies run a fashion show,
Wings in colors, oh-so-glow!
'What's in style? A flower crown!'
And daisies blush, they can't back down.

Each squirrel dons its jaunty hat,
Mustache twirls — imagine that!
The forest bursts with laughter bright,
In their world, all's pure delight!

The Arboreal Enchantment

Beneath the branches, shadows dance,
Tools of gnomes, all in a prance.
'This twig is mine!' a hedgehog shouts,
While laughing mushrooms flit about.

The raccoons have a bandit scheme,
Sneaking snacks—they plot and dream.
'That apple looks like quite a prize!'
They giggle, swapping hungry eyes.

A chipmunk's hosting tea for two,
With cookies made of leaves and dew.
'Best served with a side of cheer,'
They toast with acorns, spread the sphere.

When sunlight filters through the trees,
Caterpillars join the breeze.
What's that rustling? Just a hare!
Oops, it's me who made the scare!

Whispers Beneath the Moss

Underneath the mossy bed,
Frogs recite what they have read.
'Ribbit, ribbit, mystery thud,'
With a splash, they start to flood.

Crickets chirping out of tune,
Trying to impress the moon.
'Is my pitch too high or low?'
While owls snicker down below.

Twirling leaves in autumn's flow,
Dance like no one's watching though!
Squirrels lose the nut they hid,
'Who knew this was a dance so bid?'

Gnarled roots hum an ancient song,
Whispering where the critters belong.
In the darkness, all's a jest,
In this mossy land, they know best!

Diaries of a Silent Witness

On a bench of bark, I sit and read,
The diary of a shy old seed.
'Twas once a sprout, bright and spry,
Now just wishes to know why.

Grasshoppers leap with such cocky flair,
While butterflies float without a care.
'The tricks we played when we were spry,'
The seedling mutters with a sigh.

One wise tree shares tales so grand,
Of the neighbors, both quirky and bland.
Laughing at the passing crow,
'What a fuss, for an old show!'

In the heart of this green-domain,
Laughter bubbled like summer rain.
With plenty of sun and less of gloom,
The seat of tales will always bloom!

Ode to the Silent Sentinel

In the forest stands a tree,
Guarding secrets, wild and free.
Squirrels chatter, making bets,
While the owl snoozes, no regrets.

Leaves whisper tales of ancient lore,
Of kids who carved and dared much more.
Branches wave as if they jest,
'Tree poses better than the rest!'

One day a raccoon, quite a prankster,
Thought he could be the tree's champion dancer.
But tripped on roots, oh what a sight!
Now the tree laughs each day and night.

So here's to trees, not all stoic,
Their humor's sharp, sometimes heroic.
Next time you pass, give them a wink,
You never know what trees might think!

Dance of the Fluttering Petals

In springtime's breeze, petals soar high,
A flower's dance, oh me, oh my!
Bumblebees buzzing, caught in the fun,
Trying to keep up, but they're on the run.

Petals twirl like a feathered hat,
Getting tangled with a curious cat.
Laughter echoes through the blooming field,
Nature's charm is an endless yield.

A daring kite takes a wild dive,
Turning sweet spring into a beehive!
Petals scatter—oh, what a mess!
Still, all join in, it's anyone's fest!

With each new whiff of fragrant delight,
Flower dancers twinkling in the light.
Nature's own carnival, wild and free,
Spreading joy, just wait and see!

Legends of the Woodland Watcher

Pinecone tales that make you grin,
Of woodland watchers, let fun begin!
They spot the rabbits with curious eyes,
While pretending not to hear their lies.

A wary fox, tiptoeing through,
Stumbles on moss, oh what a view!
The trees chuckle, hiding their glee,
In this playful wood, everyone's free.

Ode to the gatherings, be it rain or sun,
Squirrels debating who's faster, such fun!
Branches sway like an old-time reel,
Claiming the title of 'trees with appeal'.

So imagine the banter on a summer's night,
When shadows blend with the soft moonlight.
The woodland's legends aren't etched in stone,
But shared in laughter, the great unknown!

The Embrace of the Twisted Trunks

Twisted trunks stand side by side,
With crooked grins, they take great pride.
A duo dancing under the sun,
In their embrace, the world's more fun.

Vines wrap tight, giggles they weave,
Together they craft tales to believe.
"Watch out for storms," one trunk declares,
The other just shrugs, "Who cares? Who cares?"

A bird on a branch starts to sing,
"Hey, trunks! You're a comical thing!"
With rustling leaves, they start a jest,
A trunky riddle: who poses best?

So laugh along with nature's crew,
Where twisted trunks give a funny view.
In this charming grove, chuckles abound,
With every glance, a smile is found!

www.ingramcontent.com/pod-product-compliance
Lightning Source LLC
Chambersburg PA
CBHW051633160426
43209CB00004B/624